EXTREME WEATHER

WILDFIRES

NORWOOD HOUSE PRESS

JACK WILLIAMS

Cataloging-in-Publication Data

Names: Williams, Jack.
Title: Wildfires / Jack WIlliams.
Description: Buffalo, NY : Norwood House Press, 2026. | Series: Extreme weather | Includes glossary and index.
Identifiers: ISBN 9781978576803 (pbk.) | ISBN 9781978576810 (library bound) | ISBN 9781978576827 (ebook)
Subjects: LCSH: Wildfires--Juvenile literature.
Classification: LCC SD421.23 W555 2026 | DDC 363.379--dc23

Published in 2026 by
Norwood House Press
2544 Clinton Street
Buffalo, NY 14224

Designer: Rhea Magaro
Editor: Kim Thompson

Photo credits: Cover, p1. Alaskagirl8821, Maria Awais/Shutterstock.com; p. 5 Quantum Hydra/Shutterstock.com; p. 6 Frame Craft 8/Shutterstock.com; p. 7 Snap2Art/Shutterstock.com; p. 8 Alex Van Aken/Shutterstock.com; p. 9 Fabrizio Maffei/Shutterstock.com; p. 10 Kyla Metzker/Shutterstock.com; p. 12 Robert Wilder Jr/Shutterstock.com; p. 13 K-FK/Shutterstock.com; p. 14 Gorodenkoff/Shutterstock.com; p. 15 Ringo Chiu/Shutterstock.com; p. 16 Tong_stocker/Shutterstock.com; p. 18 David Pereiras/Shutterstock.com; p. 20 Sergey Uryadnikov/Shutterstock.com

Printed in the United States of America

CPSIA compliance information: Batch #CWNHP26: For further information contact Norwood House Press at 1-800-237-9932.

TABLE OF CONTENTS

Watch Out! 4

What Is a Wildfire? 6

Why Are Wildfires Dangerous? 12

How to Stay Safe 19

Glossary 22

Thinking Questions 23

Index 24

About the Author 24

WATCH OUT!

Glowing flames roar. They spread through the treetops.

Watch out! It is a **wildfire**.

WHAT IS A WILDFIRE?

A wildfire is a large fire that is out of control.

It can happen in forests and fields.

A fire needs three things to burn. It needs heat, **fuel**, and **oxygen**.

Something hot **ignites** the fuel. Oxygen in the air keeps the fire burning.

The heat for a wildfire can come from **lightning**. It can come from a campfire.

The fuel can be dry leaves and grass.

WHY ARE WILDFIRES DANGEROUS?

Some wildfires are good. They clean up forests. They get rid of dead leaves and other **debris**. They return **nutrients** to the soil.

When a wildfire burns for too long, it is dangerous. A fire can **destroy** anything in its path. It can burn buildings and farms.

Smoke from a wildfire can be deadly.

People and animals have trouble breathing.

HOW TO STAY SAFE

Watch the weather **forecast**. It will tell you if there is fire danger.

Follow directions. You may need to **evacuate**.

Soak your house and yard with water.

Cover your mouth and nose to keep out smoke.

GLOSSARY

debris (duh-BREE): old and unwanted items

destroy (dih-STROY): to ruin something completely so it cannot be used anymore

evacuate (i-VAK-yoo-ate): to leave a place quickly because of danger

forecast (FOR-kast): a report that tells what the weather will be like in the future

fuel (FYOO-uhl): something with stored energy that is released as heat when burned

ignites (ig-NITES): catches fire; sparks

lightning (LITE-ning): a flash of light in the sky when electricity moves between clouds or between clouds and the ground

nutrients (NOO-tree-uhnts): minerals and vitamins that living things need to be strong and healthy

oxygen (AHK-si-juhn): a gas found in the air that has no color, taste, or smell

wildfire (WILDE-fire): an uncontrolled fire that burns a wide natural area

THINKING QUESTIONS

1. Where can wildfires happen?
2. What can supply the heat to start a wildfire?
3. What can supply the fuel for a wildfire?
4. How can short wildfires be good?
5. How can you tell if there is danger of a wildfire?

INDEX

buildings 14

campfire 11

evacuation 19

forest 7, 12

fuel 8, 9, 11

heat 8, 11

leaves 11, 12

smoke 17, 21

ABOUT THE AUTHOR

Jack Williams is curious about all things in nature, especially the weather! He checks the weather forecast every day. He used to be a police officer, so he knows how important it is to watch out for danger and stay safe.